MILITARY BRATS

Well-Traveled Lives

{SECOND EDITION}

LAURA N. NICHOLS

Illustrated by Neda Akgun

Military Brats: Well-Traveled Lives (Second Edition)

Copyright © 2024 by Laura N. Nichols

ISBN: 979-8-9920332-0-5

Nichols Blossom Press

Printed in the United States of America

ACKNOWLEDGEMENTS

This book was written to enlighten the lives of military children and those who have impacted the lives of military dependent children, often called military brats. It is also dedicated to the memory of my parents' lives—a father who served in the military, drafted from high school to serve in the Korean War and also the Vietnam War, twice. My mother, a military spouse, who sacrificed her life to support the soldier she married and her children. Both parents passed away at young ages, mom first at age 47 from colon cancer, and then dad at age 55, probably due to his hard life serving in wars, when PTSD was not yet recognized.

This book is dedicated to both parents, who always gave me the courage to be my own person and who always told me I could become anything my heart desired in life, if I worked hard. Dad always told me, "Be the best in every classroom, nothing less!" As an educator, I extended that foundation to all my students, that each was the best and had a gift to impart to the world.

I also dedicate this book to my younger brother, Bill, a high school Choral Director at Chaparral High in Las Vegas and opera singer in Henderson, Nevada, who suddenly passed away at the onset of the Covid-19 pandemic on January 4, 2021. By that time, 77,456 people had died from Covid-19 and their names were placed on flags at the Washington National Mall grounds. Bill's name and service were posted on one of those flags. He forever encouraged me to write about my experiences and to share my knowledge with the world. I will continuously be grateful for how he shared his gift of song with the students, having grown up as a military brat, born in Camp Zama, Japan. He was my educational cheerleader and trailblazer, speaking over six languages and spreading music, the universal language, throughout the world.

To my two sisters, I could not have had the drive to complete this book without your daily encouragement and prayer. I am forever grateful for your sisterhood and the wonderful memories of growing up together in a military life.

To my retired military spouse, Chaplain (LTC) Retired, USA, Delton Nichols, the love of my life. Thank you for the many military experiences that continued after my military upbringing and especially, the ability to move and teach across this global world. I am better because of you!

To my high school teacher from Fort Knox High School, Ms. Carolyn Hicks, I became an educator and leader with confidence due to your belief in me and telling me I had a talent and a gift! A teacher envisions the best for every student, you did that. Your example of being a female teacher and African American, in the area of physical science and mathematics on the high school level in the 1970s was rare. Your illustration of the future for each of us was impactful. I am thankful for the value you placed on my education.

To Dollye Smith, my mentor and cheerleader in life. You became my new mother, upon the passing of my parents. Every step of the way, you have encouraged me to live my dreams and to make a positive difference in the world. I am grateful for your continual love and support, even to the present.

Finally, I could not have this story to tell without my two wonderful, talented, creative, and gifted daughters, Tiffany and Darian. My life with both of you encouraged me to write and tell about the impact of military children in the world. I know both of you have made a huge impact on the lives of others, as a result of your military life, despite living through the eclectic changes and sacrifices. Thank you for always being the best daughters any father and mother could have. I wish both of you many more years, sharing your global experiences and knowledge with others and making a difference throughout our world. You make me a better person.

Most of all, I am indebted to Kate Winter for believing in my message and leading me to a finished version. This would not have happened without her keen eye and professionalism. I thank her for believing in this educator and the story that could be told.

CONTENTS

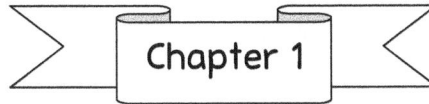

Chapter 1

LEARNING FROM MOM

Growing up, I was told that I was not just any "ole" child. I was a special kind of offspring on this Earth. I was what one calls a "Military BRAT!" I always heard people call me that name, but did not know why. I asked my mom, "Why do people call me a military brat all the time? When we go to the commissary, I hear people speak to you directly and they use those words. Mom, what is a military brat? Why do people call me names like that? It makes me feel bad. Can you answer my question?"

"Well," she said, "let us sit down and have some milk and chocolate chip cookies, while I tell you about what it means to be referred to as a military brat and what honor that entails." So, I sat down at the table as she began explaining. "People don't mean any harm when they say the name, 'military brat.' They are words meant to explain a very exceptional group of kids. They are children who have seen more in the world around them than the children who don't have parents in the military. Many of their parents have done something special to help keep freedom in the world."

This book shares the lessons my mom taught me about what it means to be part of this unique group, and my own adventures growing up as a military brat.

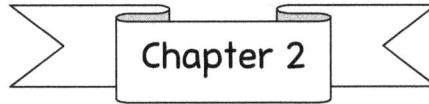

Chapter 2

HISTORY OF MILITARY BRATS

The term "military brat" goes way back in history to a time when British soldiers used the name to describe their families. The British soldiers served abroad and could take their children to live with them, wherever they were stationed, lived and worked, in another country such as India. People began to use this term to keep records of the families. They were named BRAT (British Regiment Attached Traveler). The name was not meant to be mean. It was used to describe this group of children. As a result, people in the world remembered this term and started using it for many years. It is a term that is no longer used officially; however, history was made and many military dependents still use the term, but in a respectful way.

"Your sisters and brothers are special, too!" my mom told me. "Each of your siblings was born in a different place in the world: Japan, New York, New Jersey, and

Germany. Your sisters and brother were born on a military base, and your dad is a military soldier. You are that unique and awesome kind of child! You are not like others, some who live in one place all their lives. You are a GLOBAL, well-rounded person. The world is better because of you and the experiences you have."

Military brats are children who have one or both of their parents, or a guardian (a person who cares for them as a parent) serving or working as an active soldier for the military or in the reserves. The military is the organization or company under which one or both of their parents work. If a parent is on reserve active duty, they may work a military job from time to time. Sometimes, it can be a full year or more, depending on the world and whether it is wartime. During those times, they can work as a full-time active duty soldier.

A parent can be in either the Navy, Army, Marines, Coast Guard, Air Force or National Guard. They work in all types of jobs: doctors, sergeants, nurses, trainers, supply, scouts, intelligence, authors, chaplains or ministers, engineers, pilots, tankers, air traffic controllers, admirals, computer analysts, technology, dentists, authors, news reporters, and many other careers.

The Navy was important in helping families move abroad or overseas. Families traveled from one duty station to another on a large military ship or ocean liner. I came to America at the age of four on a Navy ship, the *USS W. A. Mann* (T-AP 112). It was special, almost like a cruise ship. We were on the ship for two weeks. In the 1960s, military families traveled from America to other bases in another country on these Navy ships. The ships had sleeping rooms, a large dining hall, and places to listen to entertainment, or a special show. My mom always said, "It was a two-week cruise." This was before the average person — not only very wealthy — traveled on commercial ships or cruises.

Our ship crossed the seas at 50 North Latitude and 180 Parallel in July 1959. All families were given a certificate when they crossed the 180th parallel, the International Date Line. This was a historical event and special time only a military child experienced. I was four years old and am now a product of this American history. I even have an authentic certificate to show I traveled across the Prime Meridian on that ocean liner. The Golden Dragon Certificate was given to soldiers and dependent children, who accompanied their military soldier. In a certain sense, one is entering the Dragon Empire when they cross to the west.

The *USS W. A. Mann* was used in other situations, carrying dependents to transport gold and silver, along with a special letter for the President of Korea, prior to this time period. Also, it was utilized for many other missions. The military families in the 1950s and 1960s were carried across the Pacific to Asian countries and Europe.

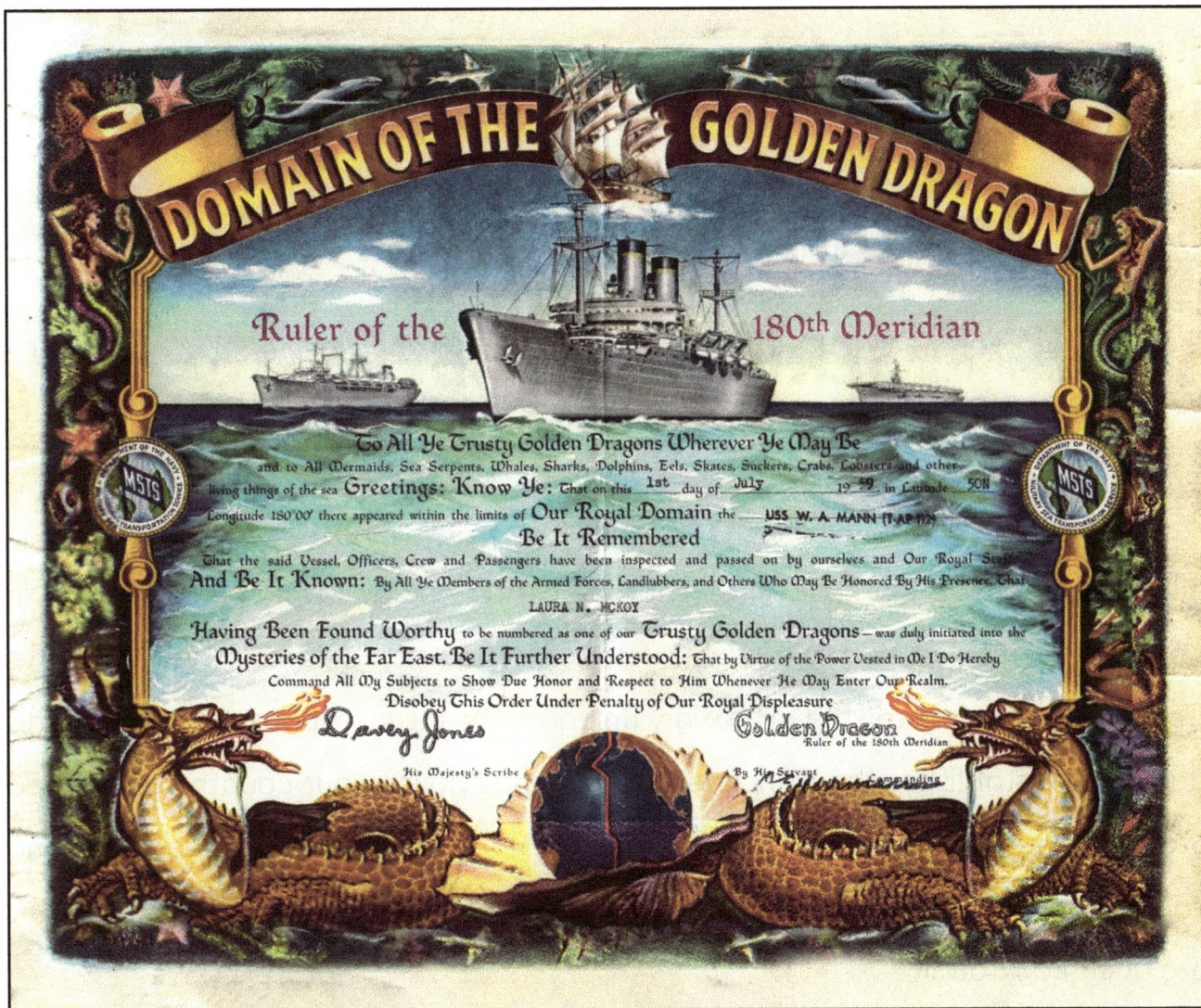

Certificate given to military dependents and family members when they crossed the 180 Prime Meridian. This picture shows a certificate from July 1959 given by the captain of the *USS W. A. Mann*.

Chapter 3

IMPORTANCE OF MILITARY SERVICE MEMBERS

All military soldiers work full-time to protect the freedoms which each person in America is entitled to have. These freedoms are found in the United States Constitution. They are listed in the very first part, the Introduction or Preamble. This document establishes the principles or rules that govern our country, the United States of America. The soldiers work to help establish justice. Justice means treating each person fairly and doing what is right, proving someone is innocent when they are accused wrongly.

In addition, our soldiers work to ensure there is peace in America. They also work to provide defense or protection to America and the countries in which we have military bases and their families or dependents. Most of these countries have a democracy and are free, providing for our common defense. Our soldiers work with other countries to move towards world peace and democracy. For example, there are soldiers in Germany, Japan, Italy, Guam, South Korea, and many other territories.

All soldiers have a major task or duty. That is to provide for the common defense, protecting our nation from attack. Every soldier works to help with issues of poverty, housing, food, and economic or social welfare. Sometimes soldiers go to places to help American citizens with problems that happen in these areas.

In our current day, soldiers have gone to help American citizens when called upon by the government or president to help. In the United States, each state has a National Guard of soldiers who are ready to go help and provide support with these problems and conditions. In the present day, National Guard soldiers are helping with the influx of immigrants coming to the US through Texas. There is a National Guard in each state and US Territory. The National Guard is called to go and support people with difficult situations, such as: disasters, hurricanes, tornadoes, earthquakes, tsunamis, typhoons, oil spills, fires, other types of destruction, and overwhelming health needs when hospital staff can't provide support on its own. They also help with humanitarian efforts to provide food, shelter, and medical support. Their main mission is to protect and defend! They share a motto: "Always Ready, Always There." Many of the National Guard soldiers serve as reserve soldiers or as active duty. When they are active duty, their families live the same as active military families.

Whenever these situations occur, military brats or dependents of military soldiers' families have to sacrifice and separate from their loved ones who leave home to help on these many missions. You are special, all part of the connection with being a military child, with parent(s) who give of their lives daily, sacrificing time that could be spent with their own families. The average citizen does not have to see their parent or parents leave home for small or large amounts of time, sometimes for even a year or two. Many occasions may be for dangerous situations or missions, such as wartime or to rebuild an area. Military children are extraordinary. They endure or live through far more changes than the average citizen or child. They are strong and love all humankind. This makes them superb and resilient. Military children are respectful of their parents' commitment to freedom.

A military service member enjoys spending time with his daughter.

Many children who have parents in the military are patriotic. They understand the flag and its symbol for freedom and the rights we have in the Constitution. You can find military children singing the songs for all of the armed forces. When I was in school, our music teacher taught us all of the patriotic songs. When that flag waves, the songs are imprinted in my mind and the singing begins. Most Americans see this when they watch the Memorial Day services on television or visit the Capitol on the Fourth of July in Washington, DC. The music plays the patriotic songs and the bystanders place their right hands over their hearts and if a soldier is in the crowd, they automatically salute to give reverence or respect to the soldiers who serve, have served, or died in the line of duty, while in the military.

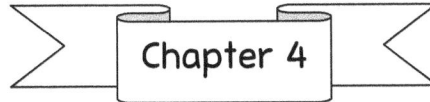

Chapter 4

MILITARY SERVICE MEMBERS AND FAMILIES ADJUST IN THE WORLD TODAY

During 2019, a new pandemic, the Coronavirus (Covid-19) began. A pandemic is where a disease occurs which is infectious and has spread rapidly across large regions and worldwide. Our soldiers immediately traveled and worked in many places across the world to help slow and to try to stop the spread of Covid-19. Consequently, their families had to adjust again to their loved one(s) being exposed to the virus and working long hours to help others. In many cases, the military soldiers had to leave their families to travel across the world and throughout the

United States to assist and support the world in hopes of finding a cure and healing the multitude of Covid-19 cases spread throughout the world.

With the president at the time (2020-2021), President Donald Trump, invoking the Defense Production Act, military soldiers worked on the naval ships *USS Comfort* and *USS Mercy* to help with the excessive amount of Covid patients and deaths occurring daily during the pandemic, along with dispensing immunizations in record speed. The sacrifices required of military families occurred again. Despite these continued sacrifices and changes in their lives, military children continue to be open-minded and versatile. The military soldiers' patience, expertise, and sacrifice from their families helped many American citizens live through this impactful time.

Once again, the military brats had to adjust to saying farewell to their parent(s) as they traveled away from home to help promote tranquility and general welfare for others. That makes military children magnificent, and incomparable to any other children. They are resilient and compassionate, caring for others. They go through life and face unreal situations, other kids do not! Sometimes the situations occur without any preparation. If the parent works with special forces, the children may not even know where their parent is going or when they will return. Our soldiers also secure liberty or freedom for American citizens in the world today and for future posterity!

Every American depends on our military to help us to be able to live freely. We can go where we want, do what we want, and say what we believe through peaceful protests. You can't do this in a country that is not free. In countries without freedom of speech, people and citizens are not able to speak what they believe, worship where they want, or travel freely. It is because of our magnificent soldiers and their families and their support that these freedoms in America and its territories abroad occur. The military child encourages their military parent to continue. Every military soldier wants freedom for his country and family! It is the family that sets the framework and foundation to give the soldier the drive to continue and to make this world a better place for all humankind.

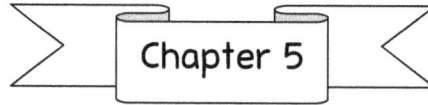

Chapter 5

MILITARY PROMOTES FREEDOM

In America, citizens can protest peacefully and freely, if we don't agree. We can go to whichever church, synagogue, temple, or mosque with our own free will. In a country with a dictatorship, where one person rules the entire country, people are unable to listen to whichever news station or use any media platform they want. They are unable to protest if they don't agree. They do not have control of the constitutional laws. One person, who is authoritarian, rules the country and the ways of life for the people. In countries where there is no freedom, people often hear news that is not factual, but propaganda or untrue. Every person can thank our military soldiers for supporting and protecting these freedoms in the United States and its territories, and at bases throughout other countries.

Equally important, the soldier's children, the military brats, sacrifice by not seeing their parent in times of war or movement. The children may have to move all over the world with their parent to support this American right of freedom. Sometimes, the move may be in the middle of a school year and new friends have to be made. Military children adapt and learn to get along with others. Military kids are AWESOME!

My mom pointed out, "Laura, you went to over three high schools. This is not the same as graduating from a high school where you know everyone and all the teachers know you. Despite this, you graduated with honors. You are special and part of an esteemed group of children, military brats, making a difference throughout the world."

Chapter 6

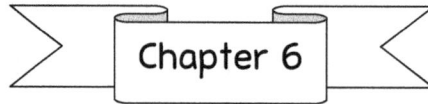

GROWING UP AS A MILITARY CHILD

Growing up as a military dependent is very unique and interesting. One has the best of both worlds—a time for learning and a time to sacrifice. You have the chance to spend family vacations in the host country, the country where you live. When I was a military child, we traveled to Nikko, Japan. The family would vacation on ski trips and then go on additional trips to visit the grand city of Tokyo, a city bustling with activity, vivid Japanese cultural sites, and scrumptious food with Japan's exquisite cuisine.

My mom reminded me of the unique experiences I'd had. "Laura, our family would travel wherever we lived. I always liked the weekend excursions to sightsee famous castles and old cities in Germany such as the Neuschwanstein Castle or Trier. Who can live this real educational life other than the wealthy? The military is fortunate

The famous Neuschwanstein Castle nestled in the Bavarian Alps in Germany

to have these opportunities readily available. You are special and fortunate, embarking on the treasures the world has to give, real-life knowledge. While you were living in Germany, you were able to travel to Vienna, Austria to see Mozart's piano. You had the opportunity to really learn about other countries, not just for a week or two, but for years at a time! This is not the same as traveling on a cruise or traveling on a vacation for a week or two. You were able to see and live a life in these places for long periods of time. When you live in an area for quite a while, you get to learn the full customs and ways of living."

"Military children gain a vision of real pictures of places and can learn the authentic culture, even the language. That is what makes a military child global and world-minded! Military children are the best the world has to offer. I am proud to be part of this family and you should be, too."

She continued, "You were born in Germany, which means abroad in another country, but you are still a United States citizen. You have two parents who were born in America—in New York and North Carolina. There are many military children or dependents, children born to parents who are enlisted and serve in the military. These children may be born in other countries such as Germany, Belgium,

Japan, Korea, Italy, and throughout the world, along with the variety of states in the United States of America. They are called naturalized citizens; born outside the United States, but they obtain citizenship."

"Some military children are born in a military base hospital. There are military bases in many states for the Army, Navy, Air Force, Coast Guard, and Marines. Not all children are born in these hospitals, but many military kids are! You were born at the United States Air Force (USAF) Hospital in Wiesbaden, Germany and your brother in Zama American Hospital in Zama, Japan. Another relative was born in the largest military hospital, Landsthul Regional Medical Center, Landsthul, Germany. That is so very special! The Landsthul hospital takes care of major sickness, trauma, injuries, and ailments that soldiers from war zones and other areas of Europe and Asia experience. It still exists today! The most intricate situations are sent to Landsthul. It is one of the most famous military hospitals and they were delivered there! How remarkable is that?"

Military children are born all over the world—in hospitals off-base in addition to military hospitals—and live in many different communities. Most military children live in more than five different places. This makes them very resilient, versatile,

The Alexander T. Augusta Medical Center, formally called Ft. Belvoir, located in Fort Belvoir, Virginia

transient, exceptional, and global. They are able to learn how to be global citizens, people who can adapt and share different ways of life and culture. Military children learn how to get along with many different cultures and treat people with respect. They understand what is considered proper and respectful for different cultural groups and how to greet each culture and adapt to their living styles and values.

In the military base schools, students have a Host Nation teacher, a teacher specializing in the language and culture of the country. The students learn basic language skills for that country and the living customs and ways of life. Along with instruction, they participate in related field trips and celebrations for the country they live in. Most military children go to school on a military base when they live in another country with their military parent(s). In some American states, families can live on base or off base. As a result, many military bases, not all, have schools on base for elementary, middle, and secondary levels. Within the last few years, many children now go to a county school near the base. This has been cost-effective for the government.

The schools on federal property are called Department of Defense Education Activity (DoDEA) schools. There are a few in the United States of America in places like Quantico Marine Base, Fort Jackson, Fort Campbell, Fort Hood (now Fort Cavazos), Fort Benning (now Fort Moore), and Fort Knox, to name a few. I went to Fort Knox High School, "Home of the Eagles," in Fort Knox, Kentucky for a few years. There are many other schools throughout America from East to West Coast and North to South. Schools are also overseas in areas such as Europe, the Pacific, and the Americas, throughout the Army, Navy, Air Force, and Marine territories.

Military children are taught by well-certified and degreed teachers in these schools. Each school curriculum follows similar studies with a major core curriculum. In addition, there are sports, STEM, foreign language, and other high academic programs. The dependent military school environment is different from going to a school in a typical civilian United States school. The children journey on field trips and see authentic places in foreign lands. The field trips are extensive. The schools are eclectic, there is diversity with students enrolled with many cultural backgrounds and experiences.

I was able to see many famous sites in Japan when we lived there with my school, such as the gigantic Buddha in Kamakura, Ueno Zoo, Mount Fuji, Imperial Palace, and the Children's Peace Memorial in Hiroshima, to name a few.

24

The Children's Peace Memorial in Hiroshima, Japan

The famous Ueno Zoo located at Taino City, Tokyo, Japan

26

Consequently, textbooks came alive through the life I lived. For example, when I read *Sadako and the Paper Cranes* (a historical novel about a young girl, written by Eleanor Coerr in 1977) it stayed forever vivid in my mind. I could make connections to the places where I actually went sightseeing. I have also seen the peace memorial for the lives lost in Hiroshima. The Children's Peace Memorial was inspired by Sadako and her paper cranes.

I once toured the Ueno Zoo with my class. I could observe the giant pandas and exotic animals from Central Africa and Zaire. It is one of the most visited zoo sites in the world and legendary for the variety of unique animals housed there. In addition, I learned about the sad tale of the elephants at the Ueno Zoo, who died of starvation due to World War II, and how the zookeepers did not want this to happen. This was written about in the book *Faithful Elephants* by Yukio Tsuchiya.

These sites helped me understand the tragedy of war, how it impacts people and animals. Not many children in America can say they have seen these places. Both of these books have book-to-book and world-to-world connections. This enabled me to remember and extend my learning. I saw these memorials and pictures with my very own eyes. I did not have to rely on the pictures in the book, the vivid viewing of the site is forever etched in my brain, such as the clearness of a sight when looking through binoculars. My connections, book-to-world, are real! I can now share these experiences with others, so they can learn about the impact of war.

In my classes in Japan, I learned how to fold origami paper cranes at an early age, in third grade. That is something I would not have experienced in America, at this magnitude, so early on. As a military child, I could explain to others the true meaning of the paper cranes and their purpose, as I shared in my class upon returning to the USA. Everything is real to a military child. Not only was origami used for art, it was used in geometry classes to help students learn about angles, symmetry, fractions, and to problem solve mathematical equations.

I also observed the mesmerizing, intricately trimmed bonsai trees at the famous Imperial Palace in Tokyo, Japan. That vision will forever be implanted in my mind. This magnificent palace was built upon the Edo Castle and home to the Tokugawa shogun during his reign from 1603 through 1867. The castle was not always in Tokyo. It was moved to Tokyo from Kyoto. I was able to visit the site and gardens with my Zama Middle School eighth grade class, during our second residence or tour in Japan.

My eighth-grade class friends and I sit near the gardens at Imperial Palace
in Tokyo, Japan, where the emperor lives.

Each bonsai bush was meticulously trimmed, with beautiful ponds cascading throughout the countryside, surrounded by endless rows of magnificent cherry blossom trees. The palace is on a hill with the beautiful Chidorigafuchi Moat. Today, we have a Yoshino cherry blossom tree in our front yard in Virginia. It helps me remember the time spent in Japan. Whenever I see the cherry blossom trees circling the Tidal Basin and north of the Washington Monument in Washington, DC, the connection to the cherry blossoms in Japan is made. I know how the cherry blossom trees were given to America by Mayor Yukio Ozaki as a symbol of friendship between Japan and America. They are a small cascade of a multitude of cherry blossom trees growing throughout Japan.

The most spectacular field trip I ever went on was in Japan to the Silkworm Factory. I was in eighth grade and our class had already gone on several field trips: Imperial Palace, the Japanese American Science Festival, Kamakura, a Japanese movie studio to see the filming for *King Kong*, and on a trip on the famous Shinkansen bullet train, one of the world's highest-speed railways. It travels throughout Japan from region to region.

Our class trip was so informative and educational. Our class boarded the comfortable, commercial, fancy tour bus to Tomioka Silk Mill near Tokyo in the Gamma Prefecture. We entered the area and for acres, there were rows and rows of beautiful green mulberry bushes, each carefully grown. One could smell a certain scent, like fresh grass in the springtime. The environment also included red brick buildings.

The Tomioka Silk Mill was created during the Meiji era from 1868-1912 to help Japan modernize and use machinery in the process of making silk. Advisers from France were sent to help with the process of mechanization. As our class entered the building, a rotten sulfur smell was in the air—the stench of worms boiling. The entire class clasped their noses with their fingers. Some of my friends snickered and ooh-ed and puckered their lips and pinched their noses, as if they could stop the pungent smell! As middle-schoolers reacted, the sound of "Oo-oo-ooh" resonated through the air, our teacher echoing and gesturing for us to be quiet. Next, the class traveled to the area where the cocoons were boiled and then on to an area where the cocoons' threads were woven on gigantic weaving machines. The thread was woven into silk and spun around on spindles. The process was intricate and amazing.

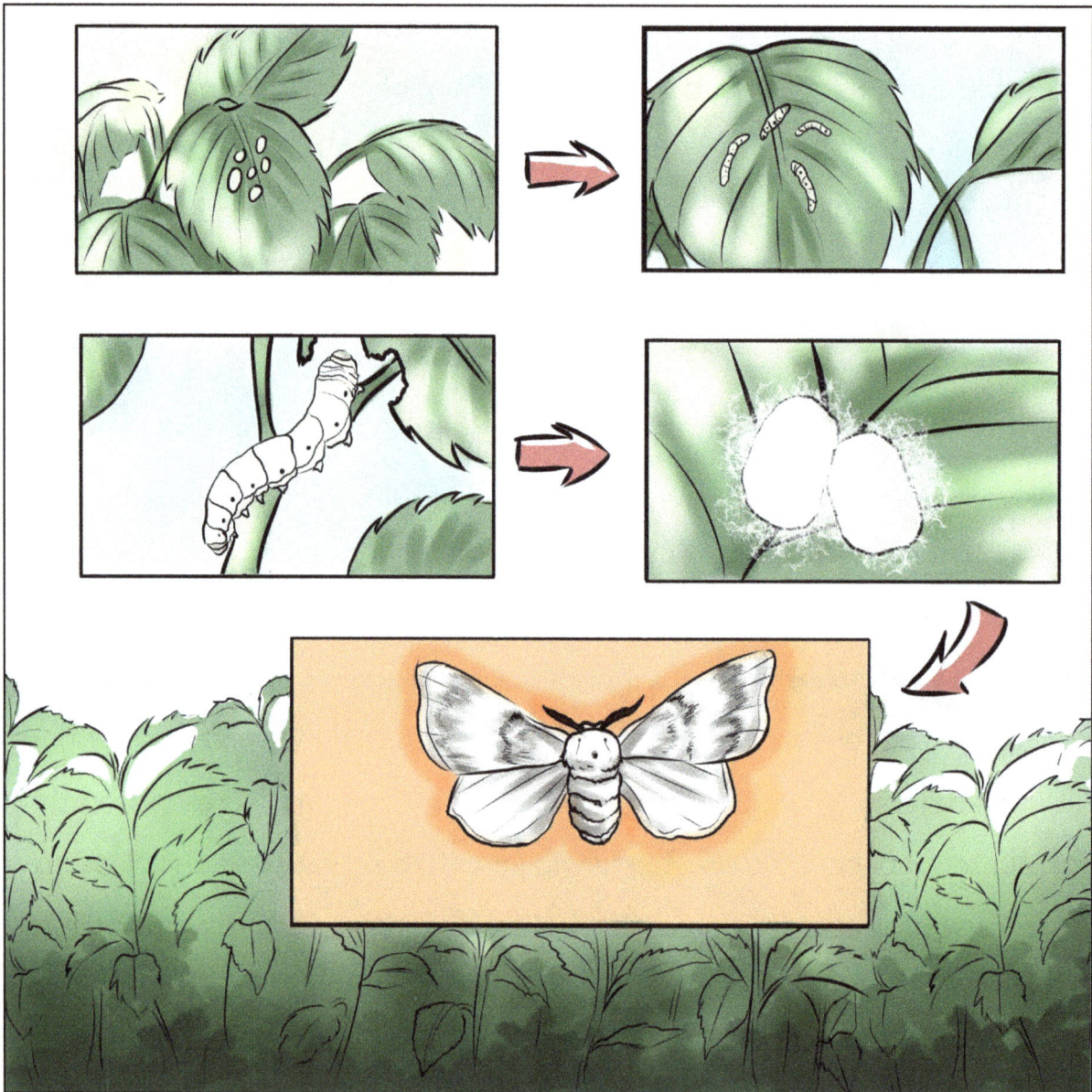

The life cycle of the silkworm was observed at the Tomioka Silk Mill.

Forever in my mind, I can see the large silkworms feeding rapidly on the mulberry leaves, workers cutting the leaves and collecting the worms, moving on to the silk-making. Just mention silk and my mind and nose sharpens, making a real life connection to the process. I am in my adult years and can still smell the scent. What a life experience! Even when I wear a silk scarf, my mind reminisces on how that silk was made. This was an opportunity one would not find in reading a book in class in the United States. One would just know the silk fabric was created. The process is intricate and intriguing. No wonder the great expense one pays for silk.

Another wonderful experience was Children's Day, Kodomo-no-Hi. It is part of a Golden Week for children. I celebrated this day in Japan every May 5. It was always filled with many activities and joy for children. Japanese people celebrate children's personalities and happiness. Japan values the joy of having children. Parents and families have part of the week off to travel, visit with other family members, spend money on children, and to just have a great amount of leisure time with their families. The holiday has changed to an entire week. Boys' Day, Tango no Sekku, used to be separate, but is now included in the Golden Week. Girls' Day, and Shichi-Go-San is celebrated in November. It is a day to celebrate children ages 3-5-7. The parents celebrate the growth and well-being of their children.

Celebrating Children's Day at Sagamihara Elementary School in Japan

Children are very special in Japan and are considered miracles. As a military child, I was able to partake in this custom. I can reflect on the giant carp fish kites flying in the air, and the festive celebration with children wearing beautiful kimonos celebrating at my school.

Every student seemed to love school. The school curriculum and learning was interesting. We were anxious to go to school everyday. I learned how to speak conversational Japanese in school. Every child was exposed to the host nation language, the language of the country one was residing in. In Germany, it was German, in Japan it was Japanese. When children are introduced to a foreign language at an early age, they learn to speak different languages with more ease. This allows them to adjust to others easily and they have the ability to communicate more readily with people that are strangers. One can meet a military person almost anywhere and strike up a conversation.

My mom explained, "Laura, that is why you love speaking to people, treating everyone with respect and dignity. These things have been embedded in the schools you attended and your home life. You are exceptional, because your life is an example for the world!"

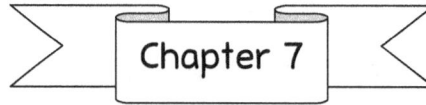

Chapter 7

MILITARY CHILDREN'S WAY OF LIFE

A military child also experiences the cultural ways of life in different countries. It may be through sampling and adding different foods and customs to your life. For instance, we make our own gyoza (Japanese dumplings or potstickers) and sukiyaki (beef with tofu and vegetables). Another custom we participate in is taking off our shoes upon entering our home. We clean our house thoroughly for the New Year. These things we learned and adapted to our lifestyle from living in Japan twice, eight years total, and practicing the cultural ways and practices, along with eating a variety of foods.

In Germany, I was able to sample lebkuchen cookies—cookies made with almonds and spices like cinnamon, nutmeg, and cloves. During Christmas time, there was the Kristkindlmarkt, all lit up with candles on real trees and beautiful ornaments!

A German village

It is the most famous Christmas Market in the world. I also learned different customs such as airing out the house daily, walking to the store, living in a German Village, Weilerbach. There were many customs and ways of living I participated in years before they became a practice in America, such as not using disposable bags, and walking to the store daily to buy necessary food items.

Military families and children also shop in stores called the Post Exchange or Commissary: the Post Exchange (PX) – Army, Base Exchange (BX) – Air Force, Marine Corps Exchange (MCS) – Marine Corps, Coast Guard Exchange (CGX) – Coast Guard, and the Navy Exchange (NEX) – Navy. These are department stores where you can buy a great variety of things, such as clothing, bikes, electronics, books, toys, furniture, some foods, cosmetics, items from other countries and places, even garden supplies. Everything is convenient under one large roof or store. They were built many years ago as a place for soldiers to shop and to buy needed items, especially when they were at war or in a country away from the United States. Military families do not pay taxes on items bought in the exchange, but they pay a surcharge at the commissary, a grocery store.

A military commissary

The commissary is a great benefit open to all military parents and their children. The store sells the same items as in a larger civilian grocery store like Giant, Publix, Harris Teeter, Kroger, Piggly Wiggly, or Wegmans, to name a few similar stores. There are many sections: produce, meat, bakery, dairy, bread, needing supplies, etc. This benefit provides items for all military personnel—active, reserve, and retired. It was also started like the PX many years ago when soldiers were stationed or had jobs away where there weren't many supplies.

Leisure time is fun in military life! Every year the military has a special "Armed Forces Day." This is a day to celebrate the lives of soldiers and their families in the armed forces: Army, Navy, Coast Guard, Marines, and Air Force. On this day, as a child, you can see unique airplanes fly overhead at an air show. I have seen the SR-71, F-15, F-16 to name a few. The show is spectacular.

In the Army, every base has a show depending on the specialty for the base. At Fort Knox, Kentucky, the tankers would bring out their military M60 tanks and let kids ride around in them. There are tents erected and opportunities at some bases to rappel like the military does in contests. I remember putting on a parachute and taking a picture with my dad.

My family celebrates Armed Forces Day at a picnic with other families.

41

It brings military life to the forefront with honor. During this day, one gets to eat and sample the most scrumptious barbecue around, play games, win prizes, get information on military jobs, and take pictures with the soldiers in their uniforms. The military songs are chanted in unison and soldiers march in cadence. It is like a huge festival! The Marines and other branches have their own Armed Forces Day activities, too. The day comes to an end with the most spectacular fireworks.

Military children also get to experience the freedom of going to the movies with their friends by walking to the theater. The price is considerably cheaper than off base and one can buy treats at a little snack shop, called a Snack Bar. Snack Bars are usually on bases overseas. In America, it is just a deli or fast food store. These days, most military bases and those in foreign countries have a McDonald's, Popeye's, Subway, Burger King, and a Starbucks. The life has changed to what is similar to American fast food places in the current times. Even if one is living in Germany or countries abroad, you might find a Burger King or American restaurant. The food may be changed slightly with the cuisine in the country one lives.

My friends and I loved to buy a bag of french fries, the crinkly type, smothering them with ketchup and dropping them in our mouths. Oh, the fries were so delicious and mouth-watering! The movie theaters were always crowded when a new movie surfaced. When I was a child, the line was wrapped around the entire building, especially when the Elvis Presley movie, *Blue Hawaii*, and the Julie Andrews movie, *The Sound of Music*, were featured. Most parents lined up to see the movie *Patton* in the early 70s. That was when we were stationed at Fort Knox, which is the home of the famous Patton Museum.

Now, that is history! The internet has changed this gap in service. Families still enjoy going to the economical theaters on some bases. Many are closing in the current day and military families must go off base to view movies. What makes a military movie setting different is, right before a movie is played, "The Star-Spangled Banner" song is played and everyone puts their hand over the heart, soldiers salute, giving honor to our soldiers who serve in war time and daily to protect our freedoms! This never happens in the civilian world. Sometimes, I am the only one standing in my school class, reciting the pledge in this day and time. In the theater on base, you could hear a penny drop, with the silence and feel the respect as everyone gives reverence to the song and saluting.

Residential life on military bases is somewhat unique and safe compared to civilian homes. The military children live in homes often on base. They are called quarters. The quarters were used to house military families. A common day term would be a duplex or townhouse. The houses are joined like a townhouse or may be a single home. The military families rent the homes for the period they live and work on a particular military base. Your friends live near you. You can just play or walk with them to school and places.

However, the neighborhoods are divided by the military rank of the soldiers, called enlisted and officers. When we lived in Fort Riley, Kansas, the homes were duplexes made out of limestone. Most were erected during General Custer's time period, or in the 1920s around the flu pandemic time. The moms would work as docents at the Custer House, named after this general. Every year in early fall, there were the Custer Days. Every mom helped bake over 800 apple pies to sell for special activities and needs for soldiers. I remember helping to peel those apples with an old-fashioned pie peeler. The wonderful apple and cinnamon aroma could be inhaled throughout the neighborhood, it was like entering your home at Christmas with the smell of delicious cookies baking in the oven! The neighbors could smell the pies for four or more blocks.

On this occasion, the historical quarters were on display for families to see. The general officers always had homes filled with collectables like their childhood heirlooms and uniforms from Citadel, a college in South Carolina, or West Point, where many high-ranking officers received degrees. People called that living experience at Fort Riley, "The Life of Riley."

On Sundays, the Gothic-looking chapel would radiate with sounds of bells playing the famous poem and song, "Ode to Joy," written by Freidrich Schiller in 1785 and set to music by the German composer Ludwig van Beethoven. It was ironic that every day on the base of Fort Riley, Kansas, exactly at 5:00 p.m., everyone would stop to listen to the "Reveille." It is a song played on the bugle by soldiers. History reports a time when soldiers would cluster together for roll call, while the song was played. The song is blasted over an intercom across the base. Everyone on the base would salute and children would stand still. Most people would get out of their cars and stand to salute, while the song played. It was a tribute to the remembrance of those who have served in the military. Only a military child would know to stop and give respect for such an honor!

One childhood experience I had in Japan occurred right in our neighborhood. I would get a large paper bag and so would my friends. In our yards, there were persimmons in the summer and chestnuts in the autumn season, September through November. We would gather together and go around the neighborhood to pick up chestnuts scattered all over the ground, under the large trees. When we returned home, our bags were overflowing with chestnuts. The chestnuts had a reddish-brown smooth outer shell when they were ripe. Before they were ripe, they were covered in green spiny shells. We never picked them off the trees, for we knew when the ripe season appeared, the chestnuts dropped off the trees and were scattered all over the ground under the trees. Once at home, our mothers used them in wagashi (Japanese treats), stir-fry dishes, and rice dishes called kuri-gohan. I loved roasting them in the oven and chomping on them, oh the nutty, sweet, buttery, soft taste, reminiscent of a baked sweet potato!

Every few days, we would gather outside and pick the chestnuts. Our brown paper bags were all more than two-thirds full. When I hear the old American song, "The Christmas Song," written and published by Burke and Van Heusen in 1945 and later sung by Nat King Cole, I think of the chestnut picking and eating the wonderful chestnuts in Japan. Chestnuts are healthy and can be roasted, ground in flour,

My friend and I gather chestnuts in my yard.

pureed, and preserved in jars. One can even freeze them. Our family would eat chestnuts throughout the fall and winter season. What a wonderful Japanese way of life! Only a military family is privy to this grand moment.

One of the best opportunities is noticing a famous person in your midst. Famous people travel through military bases, especially presidents. At Andrews Air Force Base, it is not uncommon to drive or walk and then all of a sudden, you peer around and you observe in the sky or outside an airplane hangar, Air Force One, the main airplane for the PRESIDENT OF THE UNITED STATES. As a military child, one learns to spot the dummy helicopters flying around and then you know Air Force One is nearby. At Ramstein Air Force Base, there are numerous air hangars prepared for important missions. We would love seeing the different kinds of aircraft. If you live near a base like Warner-Robins, it is not unusual to hear the planes jetting through the air at supersonic speed. When that sound of the plane travels, it makes one shake, wondering what just happened. You might spot a C-5 Galaxy cargo plane, a fighter F-15 Eagle, A-10 Thunderbolt, C-141, or a sleek F-16. Watch out for the SONIC BOOM noise, as some airplanes travel at supersonic speed!

At many military installations, it is not unusual to hear the tankers shooting in the "field," as every military child calls it. This means the place where the soldiers train in the woods. The soldiers are training and preparing to continue protecting America. The sounds are like booms of a drum or electronic music, sounding with the deepest bass.

Living in a military community on base provides so many opportunities to have a well-rounded home life. My mom told me, "Remember, Laura, you grew up on several military bases. What makes it very special is that you have a choice to go to one or more swimming pools on base! There are swimming lessons and classes. Almost all military children, no matter what their cultural background, know how to swim. That is not like your dad who grew up in the deep south and did not have access to an integrated swimming pool. You had opportunities in a more equal world!"

In 2017, a military teenager, Mary Kate Cooper from Fairfax, Virginia, was the seventh honoree for the Military Child of the Year Award for Innovation. She is a Paralympic swimming, track and field athlete. She also encourages disabled children.

Military children have friends from all cultures and play with kids from different backgrounds: African-American, Caucasian, Asian, Latino, Middle Eastern, French, British, the list continues. It doesn't matter in military life. Everyone is a person and treated equally.

My mom explained, "That is what makes you have high self-esteem and the willingness to do great things in the world. You had opportunities without being treated differently. You could be your own person. Can you imagine what America and the global world would be like, if every child and family had a world like this? People would treat others with respect and dignity. The military brat has the foundation to change the world due to their life."

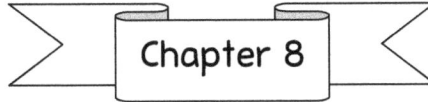

Chapter 8

MILITARY DEPLOYMENT

The military life is not always easy. There are times when my dad or mom had to say goodbye, not knowing what the future would be. This happened when my father received orders, a military transfer paper to go to war in Vietnam for a second time. This is called a deployment, when soldiers have to serve in war territories or areas that are high security. They can also go on an unaccompanied tour; there is not an option for the family to go along. My dad had already served one tour in Vietnam when I was in fifth grade. The family moved to Youngstown, Ohio for that time period. I had to go to a civilian school, Tod Elementary School, for that year.

This time, I was in ninth grade. I still remember it with a sting. We moved back to America from Japan for this. My mom did not have family to stay with, so we relocated to Roswell, New Mexico to live. There was a recently closed base at that time, called Walker Air Force Base. Over 100 families lived there, while the soldiers went to serve in Vietnam. The strangest thing is information can't be located about these families living on this base during those years. However, I have a few pictures of my family in 1969 there.

During our life at Roswell, New Mexico, we saw several of our friends cry in grief when they received news from the military about their beloved parent losing their life in war. Every military child who witnesses this, knows the sting and is frightened when you see a few soldiers, dressed in military blues or formal military dress clothing, come to a friend's house. It is the most eerie feeling, one's heart sinks to your stomach, it is like rushing up a few floors in an elevator too quickly. There is a gasp and then a scream! Everyone knows there is another loss of life due to war. Even during current times, military families feel this way when the news stations send breaking news about soldiers harmed at war. As you grow up, a military brat knows how to give honor to these soldiers for their act of freedom and unselfish life—the salute becomes more paramount and the flag a worthy symbol of freedom.

After a year in Roswell, our family prepared to move to a new duty assignment in Fort Knox, Kentucky, "Home of Armor." We were settled in our new quarters and waited daily for my dad to return from Vietnam. It was a time of restlessness. Every day, every child and parent waits with anticipation, counting and preparing for the military parent's return. It is hard to sleep through the night and concentrate at school, thinking of what your parent is going through during wartime. As a child, you are afraid and fear the unknown. The realness of war is pecking at your nerves, like a woodpecker knocking on a tree, the pecking gives you a chill and doesn't appear to stop.

To keep the connection with my dad, my siblings and I would send letters, which took a few weeks to a month to arrive in those days. We made a simple recording on a basic, condensed reel-to-reel, portable tape recorder. My brother at the young age of seven sang like Michael Jackson and belted out a few songs. Then we recorded our voices and told Dad how much we loved and missed him. In addition, our family recorded some of the famous songs played from the radio onto the tape recorder. To this day, I can hear the lyrics of many of the songs. I now know what they mean, as an adult. There were songs like, "Leaving on a Jet Plane" (Peter, Paul, and Mary, 1967), and "War" (Edwin Starr, 1970). There were so many songs about war, some against war and some about the loss of soldiers. We were sure Dad had never heard any of these songs, as time was passing quickly and he was living an entirely different life.

The United States citizens were beginning to rebel about the war, as so many soldiers were dying. Even though I was a child, a military brat, the war is implanted in my mind. It did have a huge impact on my 37-year-old dad. Yes, he was fighting a war at a young age and the impact was devastating. Our family had to endure the remnants of this terrible time in his life. Dad was never the same, when he returned. Now, as an adult, I know that post-traumatic stress took a large part of his life away.

As time passed, the year was approaching an end and Dad would soon be home. Mom helped us make signs to hang outside and in the house. She organized and decided on what special meal to make. Then the day finally arrived, the four of us jumped into our old, blue, Chevrolet Impala and mom drove us to the Standiford Airport in Louisville, Kentucky. It is now called the Louisville Muhammad Ali International Airport. Even though Louisville was only 30 miles distance from our home in Fort Knox, Kentucky, this particular day, the road seemed to be endless, like traveling through a desert looking for water. My mother was very patient, encouraging the four of us, singing songs and highlighting the sites we would see on our 30-minute trip to Louisville: Church Hill Downs, Louisville Slugger Museum, the Louisville Zoo, and Kentucky Derby Museum. Mother explained what a hot brown was, and who the latest winner of the Derby was—Secretariat at that time. This horse was the greatest winner of the second half of the 20th century. This was in the 1970s. We lived in Kentucky at that time.

As we continued on our trip to Louisville to pick up our beloved father, we entered the airport. Suddenly, everyone was quiet. What would Dad look like? It had been a year, would he know us? We were children and had written letters, sent pictures, and recorded songs. We didn't have pictures of Dad, just the ones he took prior to leaving for Vietnam. This was during the days of no social media. Generally, Dad received his letters a month later. The airport aisles and hallways seemed loud and sparkled like the spit shine a soldier would do on his or her boots. Mom led us to the gate where Dad was supposed to enter from the airplane. My siblings and I continued to wait anxiously. Mom was the most patient—having to calm four children who asked her over and over when the plane would arrive was not an easy task.

Then all of a sudden we heard an announcement for Dad's flight number. Each of us looked up at the billboard, and to our amazement, my siblings and I spotted Dad walking from the gate and carrying a duffel bag. Often soldiers travel with the duffel bags. However, at the same time, one of my sisters yelled, in a loud excited voice, "Look, there is Muhammad Ali!" Immediately, our eyes gazed in another direction to look at this famous hero, a heavyweight boxer. To our amazement, it was Muhammad Ali, "The Greatest of All Time!" We momentarily forgot Dad, and all four of us ran over to the great icon, Muhammad Ali. He looked as handsome and strong as we had envisioned from watching some of his fights on television and hearing him speak on our television. This was a chance of a lifetime, to get an autograph. Many people began lining up and waiting for an autograph. My siblings and I entered the line. Our minds had totally forgotten Dad was approaching. Each of us received our coveted autographs. Then we rushed over to the gate where Dad was.

It was like it was Christmas, reminiscent of children waiting to open a present. Our smiles were radiant, lighting up our entire faces. Mom had tears streaming and gushing down her face, enough to fill a swimming pool. It was as if she had the weight of the world lifted from her. There were other military soldiers who came off

My siblings and I wait and watch anxiously for Dad's arrival from Vietnam.

the flight, their families were also ecstatic. We surrounded our father and gave him hugs and kisses. Our father was indeed alive, he had made it back home from Vietnam! Our prayers were answered, as we prayed for his safety and health daily. DAD was back on American soil and we were now a full family again! The long year was coming to a magnificent close.

Our excitement flowed for days. The family story ended with years of dad telling each of us, "I came home from Vietnam and my family left me for Muhammad Ali." Dad was a great sport. He thought it made us a unique family, with an inspiring story to tell and a memory to remember that exact day. It also was the year when the Vietnam War ended. Our soldier, Dad, helped the world by giving his life for freedom and peace, particularly in Vietnam. As I reflect today, though I am a retired military spouse and grown dependent child, military life is embedded in my soul. I know our sacrifices made it better for others. I will always have these memories, as every military child does, too. A life well-traveled with sacrifices, unique experiences, and joy and sadness.

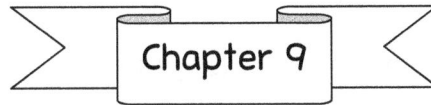

Chapter 9

MILITARY CHILDREN
MAKE A DIFFERENCE IN THE WORLD

The life of a military child gives experiences that are real and authentic; the eclectic lifestyle adds to a versatility and resilience that makes one achieve their best. There are numerous famous people who have excelled due to their military upbringing. My mom said, "Laura, you are one of these people. You have the ability to change others for the best." Then she told me about a few people who have made a difference in the world, who lived as a military child or as often stated, A MILITARY BRAT.

One very famous person who made a huge impact on life for everyone in America and globally is the famous actor, author, and podcaster, LeVar Burton. He was the famous storyteller on the PBS show *Reading Rainbow.* This television show reached a large population of children for several generations. He is also co-founder of RRKidz, Inc. Levardis (LeVar) Robert Martin Burton, Jr. was born on the military installation at Landsthul, West Germany—the exact base where one of my relatives was born. His father was an Army sergeant, who worked as a photographer for the U.S. Army Signal Corps. No wonder LeVar has made a huge difference in the world.

During that time (1980s), Germany was divided into East and West. Military families could travel from West to East Germany by riding a train called the Berlin Duty Train. This train carried USA families across the land during the night. It operated from 1945 through 1990. Each day there were several scheduled trips. The trains traveled at night, in darkness. The train carried military members, their dependents, and other official duty people. There were first and second lieutenants who commanded the trains, along with MPs (military police). There were also radio operators and an interpreter. I would often travel on the duty train to go see my sister in Berlin. She was married to a military honor guard soldier. He often helped with the military funerals and major official programs. The Honor Guard was composed of the highest caliber of soldiers.

Before we entered the train, two Russian (Soviet was the term used in 1980) soldiers would check our passports. The scary part was they would march with their strong, sequenced, stomping steps in the traditional manner you see in the old movies of Russian soldiers, depicted in the movies during World War II, the stoic faces with loud, mind-boggling stomps. The American soldiers would get off the train to watch as our papers were inspected. We would sit in fear, like a young child waiting to get your tooth filled at the dentist.

I slept in a sleeper coach or train cabin with a top and bottom bunk. The bunk could be changed into a bench to sit on, too. The trip took about 8 to 10 hours; the outside conditions were pitch black, no one could see anything. The only sound one could hear was the clicking of the wheels, striking the tracks. Just riding the train across Communist territory and seeing the Soviet soldiers ignited a fear in one's heart. Your heart felt like it skipped beats for fear of the unknown. Even to this day, when I think of the news about Russia, I reflect back on this experience. It tells me the value of freedom and how one can lose freedom in a matter of seconds.

This particular train was always utilized during the night, this way one could not see the territory outside and know what was in the Soviet territory. Most military families knew about the poverty and desolate lives in these areas. The territory was secret and sent a creepy chill up one's spine. The eerie darkness brought memories of the thriller movies one would watch. There was no sound, except the clicking of the train from time to time, and the movement of the train staff. My family and I crossed the communist territory during the evening. Usually the train would stop at two ports in Eastern Germany, the Communist area. One could hear the sound of the soldiers murmuring something in Russian and stomping, bump, bump, bump! It triggered some fear in me, there would be nowhere to go if something happened.

As you can imagine, I have images of these trips still imprinted in my mind. My trip went from West Germany across Eastern Germany to West Berlin. Remember, there was a divided Germany in the 1980s until the Berlin Wall came down. Once the train reached Berlin, Germany, the sunlight was shining and I felt relieved to be able to see daylight again. Somehow, this experience changes a person and ignites a desire to make the world a place for freedom and equality.

There are numerous military brats living throughout the world. There are famous politicians, musicians, news reporters, actors, actresses, athletes, pilots, military soldiers, educators, and authors. The list is endless. I name only a few. The *Today*

Show news anchor, Natalie Morales-Rhodes, was an Air Force brat, who lived in Panama, Brazil, and Spain. She received accolades for being one of the best morning show hosts and anchors. Suzanne Collins, the author of *The Hunger Games,* was the child of an Air Force Lieutenant Colonel who served in both Korea and Vietnam, as my father did. John Kerry, US Special Envoy for Climate (2022-Present), 68th US Secretary of State, and prior US Senator, was a military brat of a foreign service officer, born in an army military hospital. The late Senator John McCain, was born on an air base in Panama and a military brat. His life's impact is felt throughout the world. His character supported all Americans, as he lived a life in a global world due to his military upbringing. This ethic was passed on to his children and all people within his presence.

There are extraordinary military children who excel in the sports arena. Mia Hamm became one of the best soccer players from the USA. Danny Wuerffel, a famous football player, is noted as one of the University of Florida's Football Players of All Time. Priest Holmes was born at Fort Smith, Arkansas and became one of the best football players ever and the best running back of all time! The professional world-famous golfer, Tiger Woods, was a military brat and his father was an Infantry Officer, Lieutenant Colonel. Shaquille O' Neil, the Greatest NBA Player of All Time, was the son of a career officer in the US Army Reserve. The list in the sports circle continues to this day and time.

The list is also packed with famous actors and actresses, who are dependents of military soldiers. Bruce Willis, the famous actor, was born in Idar-Oberstein, West Germany. He has made the Best Actors in Film History and continues to touch the world globally with his superb talents and gifts. It is undoubtedly the foundation of his life around the military that makes Bruce global and inclusive in his work and life. Blair Underwood, a famous African-American actor, lived on many military bases during his childhood, moving with his parents in both the United States and Germany. Martin Lawerence, the famous actor and comedian's father, was in the US military. Martin was born in Frankfurt (Hessen), Germany. This is across the street from the hospital where I was born in Wiesbaden!

Mom concluded, "Laura, I could go on for days and make connections to the many military brats, in the past and present. One thing is for sure, they have made differences in so many territories and domains, to include: education, science, medicine, technology, media and broadcasting, sociology, art, ministry, diplomats, interpreters, pilots, soldiers, chefs, medicine, music, arts, drama, and every field both professionally and through service. You can look around in your current environment and you will find a person who was connected to the military."

"I am glad to have had the opportunity to tell you some of the stories of why military brats, military children, are extraordinary and world-changing people! They make a difference in how the world is viewed. They don't follow stereotypes, and they believe that every person is special and has a gift to make the world a better place. You are a proud member of that group. So, Laura, when someone calls you a 'military brat,' remember, your presence in the world is needed and you are unique, exceptional, and a trailblazer, just as the renowned people I have told you about. You come from a strong family of military brats and you can accomplish whatever you decide you want to do. You set an example for the world and all of humankind, with your global views and experience, you are the best! The difference you make can support freedom and democracy throughout the world for all cultures and citizens. Go out into the world and spread the experiences you have encountered and lived through, make the world a better place. You are a military brat with a life well-traveled. The entire human population is thankful for each and every military family and child for making a difference."

GLOSSARY

accolade – a special honor given to someone

adapt – to adjust to a situation, get use to

authoritarian – forcing strict obedience and loss of freedom

bonsai bush – a miniature evergreen tree in Japan and Eastern Asian countries, originating as an art form in China

citizen – a person who is native to a particular country and gives honor and allegiance to that country

caliber – the quality of one's character and behavior

commissary – a store on a military base, where people buy groceries

compassionate – to look after something a great deal, to feel good about something

Coronavirus (Covid-19) – a very infectious disease caused by the SARS-CoV-2 virus

constitution – the top law in the United States of America

cruise – to travel on an ocean liner or large boat

defense – to protect or resist attack

democracy – a government system where the majority of people elect their leaders, a government by the people

dependent – the family or child of a military soldier

dignity – to have honor, respect, or pride for oneself

domestic tranquility – political stability of the government, and the meeting together in peaceful protests or demonstrations

eclectic – wide-ranging, having a broad range of ideas, styles, diversity

exceptional – above average, outstanding, remarkable, superb

excursion – travel or trip

extraordinary – better than ordinary, terrific, outstanding, exceptional

global – worldwide, the entire world

justice – to treat with respect, right treatment for people

kimono – a traditional piece of clothing or garment, worn in Japan, that wraps in the front and is worn with a sash sometimes, called an obi.

leisure – free time, time to do things free from work

liberty – freedom, to be able to do as you please

mechanization – having parts to move as a machine

memorial – a tribute to someone's life or deeds

mesmerize – to surprise or make someone draw attention to you

meticulous – paying very careful attention to each detail of something, with accuracy

military brat – a person who has a parent or guardian in the military, either active or reserve duty

mission – a job or task to do

mochi – a dough-like cake made from rice, a Japanese pastry

National Guard –the military branch who works to protect the US, they are not full-time, unless they become active

ocean liner – a ship used to carry passengers across the seas or ocean

origami – Japanese paper folding

overseas – across the ocean, countries that are across the ocean

pandemic – an infectious disease that spreads across a large region

partake – to try something or participate in something

principles – rules or guidelines to follow

propaganda – information that is often not true, or biased, not founded on facts

PTSD – Post-Traumatic Stress Disorder – a disorder that occurs after someone experiences something shocking or traumatic; the person may feel stressed or afraid for long periods of time

reminiscent – reminding of something similar

renovate - to improve or change

reserve duty - duty where you serve in the military at shortened time frames and part-time

resilient - showing strength when faced with hard things

reveille - from an old French word meaning "wake up," it was a bugle call used to gather soldiers together for a meeting

reverence - to treat with deep respect

sacrifice - to give up something you like, to do without something that is needed

sergeant - a soldier who leads, a non-commissioned officer or NCO

sibling - a sister or brother

spindle - a slender rounded rod like on a stairwell

tragedy - devastation or trauma, terrible condition

transport - to move something from one place to another

typical - the usual or what is common

versatile - able to adjust and adapt to many changes

vivid - bright or clear

BIBLIOGRAPHY

Broderick, Setsu, and Willamarie Moore. *Japanese Traditions*. Tuttle Publishing, 2013.

Coerr, Eleanor, and Ronald Himler. *Sadako and the Thousand Paper Cranes*. Paw Prints, 2008.

Gibbon, David, and Smart, Ted. *Germany: A Picture Book to Remember Her By*. Crescent Book, 1978.

Jones, Devry Becker. "Berlin Duty Train - Passenger Coach." *The Historical Marker Database*, 28 Feb. 2021, www.hmdb.org/m.asp?m=167596. Accessed 17 July 2024. [Site includes picture of Historical Marker of train coach donated to Fort Eustis, Newport News, VA.]

Kirkpatrick, Tim. "Here's the History Behind 'Reveille.'" *We Are the Mighty*, 30 Oct. 2020, www.wearethemighty.com/mighty-history/history-reveille. Accessed 15 July 2024.

Lange, Katie. ""Military Brat:' Do You Know Where the Term Comes From?" *Stars and Stripes DOD News Defense Media Activity*, 14 Apr. 2017.

Montroll, John. *Animal Origami for the Enthusiast*. Courier Corporation, 1985.

Priolo, Gary P. "USS General W. A. Mann (T-AP-112)." *NavSource Online*. Service Ship Photo Archive, Auxiliaries Archive Manager: NavSource Naval History, 22 Dec. 2023, www.navsource.org/archives/09/22/22112.htm. Accessed 14 July 2024.

Stark, William N. *Mighty Military Ships*. Capstone, 2019.

Tsuchiya, Yukio. *Faithful Elephants*. Houghton Mifflin Harcourt, 2015.

ABOUT THE AUTHOR

The author, Laura McKoy Nichols, was a military child, born in Wiesbaden, Germany. She was a child of an army father, SFC (RET) William and Mrs. Thelma Bowser McKoy. Laura lived most of her early and middle childhood at a military base in Kanagawa Prefecture, Sagamihara, Japan along with her three siblings. She attended military Department of Defense elementary schools at Sagamihara Elementary School in Sagamihara Japan, and Lloyd Elementary School in Fort Benning, Georgia. Her father was drafted into the Army and served in the Korean War at a young age, right out of high school. In addition, he served two tours in Vietnam which led the family to move to Youngstown, Ohio, where Laura attended a civilian school, Tod Elementary School. Later the family transferred on another tour to Japan and Laura attended Zama Middle, which was a middle/high school combination. Then the Vietnam War led to yet another move to Roswell, New Mexico; while her father was in Vietnam, the family resided there at a "Waiting Wives Base," Walker Air Force Base, which had closed and was used for this purpose. Laura attended Roswell High School in Roswell New Mexico for ninth grade. Upon her dad's return from the Vietnam War in 1971, the family moved to Fort Knox, Kentucky, where she attended Fort Knox High for two years and then moved on to Radcliff, Kentucky where her dad retired from the Army and Laura graduated from North Hardin High School in Radcliff, Kentucky. It was there that both parents died at the early ages of 47 and 55.

Laura went on to college at Kentucky State University on an academic scholarship. She received her Bachelor of Arts in Elementary Education with honors. After which, she enrolled in graduate school at the Ohio State University and began her first teaching job at Fort Knox, Kentucky. It was there Laura met her husband, Chaplain Delton Nichols. Laura continued her military life as a military spouse, where she traveled and taught school on the elementary and secondary levels, while also working across the United States and abroad in Kaiserslautern, Germany.

Later the family returned to the United States, where she completed her Master of Education in the field of Generic Special Education at the University of South Carolina in Columbia, South Carolina and a Master of Educational Leadership from George Mason University in Fairfax, Virginia. Additionally, she completed her National Board Professional Teaching Standard Certification in the area of Early Childhood Through Young Adulthood/Exceptional Needs Specialist. Mrs. Laura. Nichols has worked as a diagnostician, teacher, and assistant principal, spanning 40 years in the field of education. She retired in 2018. She currently works as an adjunct at George Mason University. She continues to inspire others and volunteers with an international educational organization for Leading Women Educators, Delta Kappa Gamma, making an impact in education in her community and through her church. Mrs. Nichols has always valued her life as a military child and spouse. She believes that each military child has a unique story to share with the world. Through this book, she recognizes her parents' contributions and sacrifices, while giving honor to every military child and family, past, present, and future.

www.ingramcontent.com/pod-product-compliance
Lightning Source LLC
Chambersburg PA
CBHW081340090426
42737CB00017B/3229